INDIA
The Beautiful

Anthony Osmond-Evans
Foreword by Kuldip Nayar

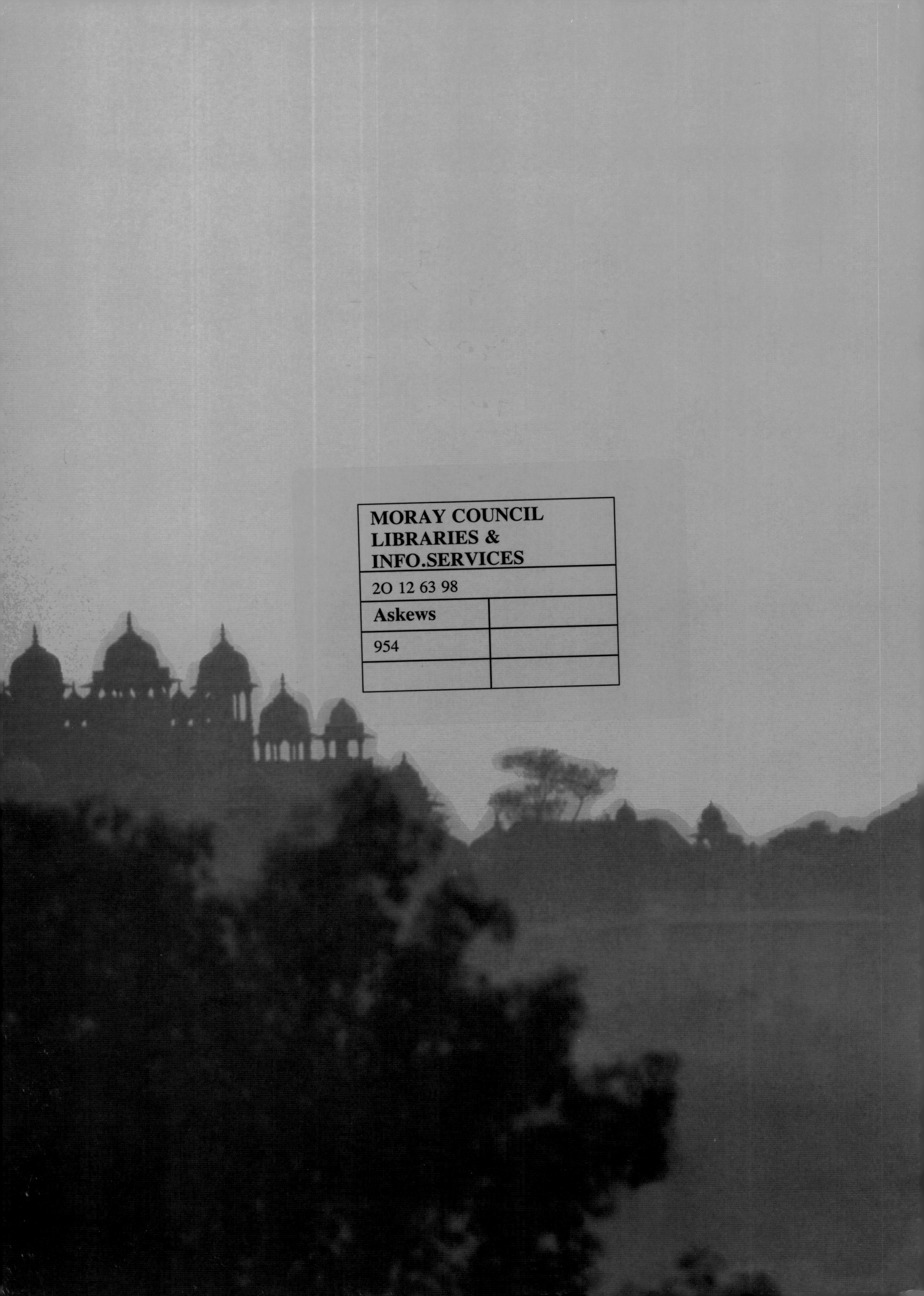

INDIA
The Beautiful

Anthony Osmond-Evans
Foreword by Kuldip Nayar

MERCURY BOOKS
LONDON

INTRODUCTION
Anthony Osmond-Evans

As a schoolboy at Tonbridge, I used to sit at a desk on which had been carved the initials 'E. M. F'. In due course, I learned that these had been inscribed by E. M. Forster, the author of the immortal 'A Passage to India'. I read the book avidly. I day-dreamed about India, never thinking that one day I would be granted the great privilege of recording that wonderful country with my camera to celebrate 50 years of Independence.

Many Old Tonbridgians have given distinguished and unselfish service to India; keeping the peace as soldiers, or assisting the maharajahs as administrators and civil servants. I came first to India on the SS Cathay in 1969, the first of many visits with neither gun nor pen, but with my camera and my artist's eyes open. I very quickly became completely intoxicated by India's rich palette of colours and soon developed a profound sense of awe of its vastness, diversity, richness of culture and the extraordinary character of its many peoples. Naturally, I viewed India from a different perspective than that of another distinguished Old Tonbridgian, Vikram Seth, who later came to my old school on an exchange scholarship and whose magnum opus, 'A Suitable Boy' has helped to give us in the West such a charming and intimate view of Indian life and culture.

As the third Old Tonbridgian in modern times to produce a book about India, my quest was to try to discover for myself the ancient essence of this fascinating country. She has been a source of inspiration and culture for thousands of years and she can rightly be called the cradle of Western language. Her beneficial influence as the source of two major world religions (Hinduism and Buddhism) has been sublime. India's discovery of the 'zero' was seminal and her influence in mathematics over two or more millennia, momentous.

Today, India has emerged as a great commercial, financial and intellectual world power, with burgeoning high-tech centres in Bangalore and elsewhere, a prosperous diamond-cutting industry in Mumbai (Bombay), which employs over one million people, and fast expanding steel and energy industries, all in addition to its renowned textiles industry. However, my overriding desire has been to record the noble timelessness of India and I therefore trust that my Indian friends will appreciate why I have not, in this present book, included photographs of the new growth industries.

Although my dear friend, Umang Hutheesing, Pandit Nehru's great-nephew, told me, "This is your book. It's your perception of India", the present work could not have been undertaken without an enormous amount of help and support, and I must particularly thank all the sponsors who have made it possible.

I must express my special gratitude to Michael Jatania, Managing Director of Lornamead Ltd and his family. Lornamead provided essential funds at the beginning, which enabled the project to proceed. Mike not only wholeheartedly joined with me in conceiving the original idea for the book, but has also been a continuous source of strength and inspiration.

Kodak, on whose film most of this book has been photographed, have played a most generous role. They have helped to arrange exhibitions in the United Kingdom and in India, and provided practical help with film and the highest quality processing of thousands of transparencies.

Kuldip Nayar is one of India's most distinguished journalists and a former Indian High Commissioner to Great Britain. In his foreword he gives us a vivid personal account of his own experiences in connection with Indian Independence 50 years ago. He eloquently combines this with a delightful description of Indian history and culture, and I am most grateful to him for all his wise advice and guidance.

Another strong source of inspiration has been the remarkable Mother Teresa. One of my most abiding memories of India was my visit to her at her home in Calcutta. I shall never forget my first meeting with this extraordinary woman, as she talked to me for over three quarters of an hour with my hands held between hers. She had the strong hands of a manual worker, short and stubby, yet gentle, and with a measure of spiritual power that was quite overwhelming. It was the calmest 45 minutes of my 53 years. My photograph of her shows in her face the life of a woman who has taken on the sufferings of the very poorest and most destitute people and given them hope, comfort and dignity.

I must pay tribute here to the vital contribution made by some of India's own great photographers. Ashok Dilwali, Prakash Israni, Samar Joda, Dr P K V Katrecha, M L Mehta, Vishnu Punjabi, T S Satyan, and the Stock Transparency Service are all represented in this book by their fine work. I am also very grateful to my own colleagues from home especially Gina Corrigan, Julian Bubb, Kim Naylor and Colin Wade. Their unique perceptions of India have added immeasurably to the depth and atmosphere of this book.

Throughout the project, my beloved companion and partner, Lorraine Felkin, has given invaluable support not only through her own photography, but also in the clarity of her

judgment in the selection of the photographs and the final design of the book. I can never repay my debt to her for her patience and generosity of spirit in putting up with my obsessive demands for excellence over thousands of miles of travel in India, and back in Jersey where we have both burned the midnight oil to bring this book to fruition.

During my travels, I have been overwhelmed, as a photographer, by many aspects of India: the rampant colours, the light and shade, the beauty of the faces, and the timelessness of the countryside where India's

heart may truly be found. It is a country ablaze with colour. The colours and styles of the saris and turbans mutate, subtly, every 26 miles. For those 'in the know', this helps to differentiate each sector. To Indians, shades and hues are infinitely interwoven. This is why this book has been laid out in the way that it has. It might appear, at first sight, to be somewhat at random, but in fact there is a thread running through, which is the interweaving and inter-relationship of colours.

Throughout my many journeys in India, particularly over the last decade, I have taken countless photographs of the great sub-continent, but I have deliberately excluded from this book any pictures of tigers, with their own distinctive and colourful livery of tawny gold and black. I have done this in order to highlight the demise of this magnificent animal. It is truly shocking that there are now only 4,000 tigers left in India, in spite of the efforts of India's own wildlife conservationists. Such is the demand in the Far East for what are believed to be the medicinal properties of the tiger, that their numbers are diminishing at the rate of one a day, with the strong possibility that these animals will be virtually extinct in less than 10 years.

While so many religions are practised peaceably side by side in India, I trust that, despite my membership of the MCC, I might be forgiven for the fact that lack of space has prevented my including any photographs of people participating in the latest Indian religion, which of course is cricket! Who in one book can do justice to India when there are dozens of volumes that could be written on turbans, saris, temples, religions, rivers, even hockey and cricket?

Pandit Nehru proclaimed at the time of Independence in 1947, "We have a tryst with Destiny". Today, this book is a tribute to the Indian people for this the 50th Anniversary of their Independence, although for me, India's nobility is timeless. She is indeed all the things that I once read and heard about, but having photographed her ancient wrinkles so intimately, this quality of timelessness has impressed me strongly, and this is what lies at the heart of 'India the Beautiful'.

As a great admirer of Mahatma Gandhi, it is perhaps appropriate that I should end by sharing with you some words I noticed on a wall in New Delhi near the Monument of the Eleven Martyrs, which has Gandhi at its head –
"There is only one India – it belongs to all of us."

TAKING PHOTOGRAPHS IN INDIA

India's vibrant colours, vast cultural diversity and many extraordinary historical sites, but above all, its light, makes it irresistible to every photographer. As you will see from the quality of the pictures in this book you can be entirely confident about using Kodak film – particularly the new Ektachrome E1OOS (the 'S stands for Colour Saturation). For me, Kodak film proved utterly consistent throughout a wide range of temperatures, from the freezing heights of the Himalayas to the heat that prevails in the rest of India.

Heat affects film. Always keep it as evenly cool as you can. Do be careful not to leave your camera or film in the hot sun, and don't forget hot ground can radiate heat into your bags. After exposure, your film should be developed as soon as possible.

When you come out of air conditioning into the heat, there could be condensation on your film and lenses. Allow them to demist naturally – do not wipe as this may damage their coatings. Take an abundance of batteries; they become harder to obtain in good condition the further afield you travel.

At airport security ask for your film to be hand searched, rather than risk the possible damage from a faulty X-ray machine.

People's eyes, usually an important element in photographs, can be obscured by shadow if you take pictures outside between 1Oam and 4pm. Fill-in flash will counteract this. To be on the safe side, take one picture with flash and one without. My own Nikon SP26 flash gun has a wonderfully sensitive fill-in flash, and gives perfect results.

Pictures taken in the early morning or late afternoon usually give richer results. The angle of the sun's rays helps to throw splendid shadows. At these times there is much more to see in the villages, as people go about their normal lives. This is equally true of the wildlife in the jungles. To capture all of this I have found that Kodak's faster Ektachrome E1OOS film, which has all the colour saturation qualities of 50ASA, works brilliantly.

I recommend the use of a tripod, particularly with telephoto lenses, to avoid camera shake and thus enable you, especially in low light, to produce superior photographs. Slower shutter speeds commensurately increase the depth of field. I use the new lightweight Gizo tripod. Amazingly strong, it collapses to virtually nothing.

In addition to my trusty Nikon 35mm F4 and F5 cameras, I also use a Mamiya RZ with Apo lenses. In my opinion, Mamiya produce the best medium-format (6 x 7mm) cameras in the world, giving unsurpassable quality. They are relatively easy to use, particularly with a special prism attachment for easy viewing. The Mamiya RZ also incorporates one of the finest automatic metering attachments of any camera. The larger format of Mamiya makes the transparencies easier to view, and the quality is particularly potent for exhibition-size photographs.

At 35mm, I usually use a Zoom 28-70mm, the 105 fixed lens macro with its close-up facility. The fast 18OED 2.8mm lens is my most useful telephoto lens. I do not like telephoto zoom lenses, but there is a very good 80-200 2.8 Nikon lens, with which as a rule of thumb you should have a minimum reading of 1/125th of a second should you be hand-holding.

Any exposure for an important subject should be 'bracketed'. I do this in thirds from one stop under to one stop over. Complex pictures with an excess of darkness or brightness should be bracketed even wider. You may not be travelling to that remote area again. At best, you obtain at least an extra, good, original picture. For prints from trans-parencies, you have a small tolerance of only about a third of a stop. With prints from colour negative film, you can print as much as two stops either way.

Time spent on reconnaissance is never more worthwhile than in India because pictures of many official ceremonies in India require official permission. You may need much perseverance to obtain this. A number of religious and secular sites and villages are forbidden to the foreigner.

Understandably, security is tightening up in all parts of the world, and in India be prepared to be disappointed if you turn up to a ceremony or an archaeological site without the correct pass. The Archaeological Institute of India does grant permisssions, but requests must be placed many months ahead. Heritage sites are becoming increasingly difficult to photograph and tripods and flash are often forbidden. You can no longer photograph the Taj Mahal by night – moonlight shots there are history. Nor can you take pictures of the tombs inside. It is therefore worth working closely with local guides, who are often able to be of considerable assistance.

Despite the many challenges, however, there is still an inexhaustible wealth of material to be photographed in India. This book merely scratches the surface.

FOREWORD: 50 YEARS OF INDIAN INDEPENDENCE

Kuldip Nayar

It is more than history. It is a saga of those who have ruled and those who have defied. India is a land of struggle and sacrifice, of suffering and subjugation, where people have sustained their identity, their being, against all odds for centuries.

Raiders came and retreated. Empires expanded and receded. Dynasties rose and retracted. India was conquered and reconquered, destroyed and disfigured. But it has remained

beautiful. Every fire has steeled it. Foreign regimes were like a gale that passed overhead, seldom disturbing the country's rhythm of life, moral codes and standards. Kings and kingdoms have never been able to intrude upon the people's privacy, their reflective thinking or their innate dignity.

Time is a mute witness to the spell that India cast on the outsiders who came to enslave it but eventually made it their home. The Allahudins, the Begum Razias or the Mughals, all were absorbed in the composite society, as the Buddhists and the Jains had been hundreds of decades earlier. The

rulers and their subjects became the warp and woof of the same tapestry, drawing strength from the different threads that had become interwoven over the years, resulting in a texture which has come to reflect diverse shades in a smooth, sturdy fashion. And as Mother Ganges has taken into her lap a multitude of different streams, whether stormy, placid or dirty, so has India assimilated the strange and the strong from several climes. Both the river and the country have remained undefiled, pure.

Some rulers, like the British, preferred to leave. Yet they carried a part of India away with them. In their drawing rooms they still display knick-knacks from the past, a sword or a bugle, or an old picture recalling how their forefathers served in a regiment stationed in some far-flung place, or lived in a district where a near relation was a deputy commissioner or a superintendent of police.

Mahatma Ghandi said that the British had to go, but were not to be driven out by violence. They were foes, but also friends. That was why the Indian bands played 'Bande Matram', the Indian revolutionary song, and then 'Auld Lang Syne' to the British soldiers as they left through the Gateway of India, Bombay, on 15th August 1947.

India itself retains the Raj in clubs and cities, cantonments and cemeteries – even cafeterias. English, the main official language of the Union, has been inherited from the British, so have our laws and our Civil Service, as well as our complex network of railways. An independent judiciary has distilled the best from the vigour and objectivity of the law courts of the United Kingdom. And the Indian armed forces retain the same British formations, combining bravery with courage.

Seldom have two peoples fought so relentlessly and yet have forgotten the confrontation so quickly. India does not remember either the excesses of her British rulers, or those who committed them. They are all history. There is no rancour. All the past, from the days of Asoka to the period of British rule, is frozen in buildings and barracks, sculptures and sanctuaries.

Such are the relics that testify to the strength of a people's fortitude and forbearance. They tell a fascinating story, not only of the architecture and artisanship that distinguishes one rule from another, but of the traditions and customs that represent every tier, every aspect of the lives of Indians. There is music and dance but also the clash of swords and the exchange of gunfire. Despite this, what pervades the atmosphere is gentle harmony matched by patience. It is revolt mingled with pain that has made the people accept even their poverty with noble resignation.

What holds people together is not religion, not race, not language, not even a commitment to an economic system. It is shared experience, involvement in the conscious effort to resolve internal differences through political means. It is a sense of 'Indianness' that unites the people of India, despite ethnic, linguistic and religious diversity.

Eighty two per cent Hindu, the country is secular and democratic. It has withstood pressure from fanatics and fundamentalists, whose fervour has always subsided eventually, because tolerance is firmly implanted in the mind of Indians. Temples, mosques and the legislative houses can string together different faiths and philosophies, but they do not mix religion with politics. The State has no church and no book other than the Constitution.

In India, even today, people look with more pride at the tall steeple of a temple or church in their community than at the chimney of a local factory. Materialism has not dazzled them. Many industrial projects, science laboratories and software plants, all symbols of modernisation are emerging in India, but they are only a few odd dots on the serene countryside that constitutes two thirds of the nation. A more familiar is the sight of village women carrying water pitchers on their heads and oxen ploughing the over-cultivated land at the call of their half-clad masters.

This way of life may give the people only a meagre subsistence, but it has the gentleness and persistence that has given the Indian a sense of acceptance rather than riches. What is happening in the industrially advanced countries has little bearing on him. He has seen them effecting changes through force, violence and war. He does not believe that any imposition is lasting. The moral aspect of development, the voluntary participation, is central to his thoughts and actions. He has always remembered the basic approach of peaceful methods. Wrong means will not lead to right results.

Mahatma Gandhi, who liberated India 50 years ago, came to the scene only in the early part of the 20th century. But his policy of non-violence, his commitment to the moral and spiritual side of life, was rooted in India's ethos, the old vedantic ideal of the life force which is the inner basis of everything that exists.

To me, India was never anything more than a geographical entity, a map daubed in pink indicating the British Empire, until I was caned by a white soldier. I was then still at school, a bystander at a protest march against foreign liquor, when I was sucked into a crowd as it was charged by lathi-wielding troops. From then on, my Country was the cause that I pursued throughout the 1930s and 40s until Partition, nay Independence, pushed me to the Indian side. I became part of that stream that flowed from Pakistan into Amritsar, 'the City of the Golden Temple'.

I still vividly remember crossing the Border. It was daylight. As I looked out, I saw people huddled in trucks and on foot passing us in the opposite direction.

They were Muslims. I saw the same pain-etched faces - men and women with their belongings bundled on their heads and their fear-stricken children trailing behind. They too, like the Hindus and Sikhs, had left behind their hearths and homes, friends and hopes. We stopped to make way for them. Some of us stood in silence to see them – just to see. None spoke – neither they nor we. But we understood each other; it was a spontaneous kinship. Both sides had seen murder and worse; both had been broken on the rack of history; both were refugees.

The first thing I did after reaching Delhi was to go to the Birla House where Mahatma Gandhi was staying. I saw him from a distance, pacing up and down on the verandah, leaning on the two girls who were supporting him on either side. I wanted to have his 'darshan', a glimpse of the person who had given India back her pride and who had released us from foreign bondage. It was his influence – and that of forgiveness – that saw the appointment of Lord Mountbatten, the last British Viceroy, as the first Governor-General of an Independent India. Mountbatten preferred that title to that of Viceroy, which he felt was associated with the Empire. It indicated a process of conciliation in the midst of the transfer of power to India and Pakistan in 1947. That trait of forgiveness has helped the nation go through the abhorrent to achieve the sublime.

When I was India's High Commissioner in London in 1990, I thought I would let the British know that we Indians bore them no ill will. I invited to India House a number of former, now ageing, Indian Civil Service and military officials who had once served in India. They had spent their best years in my country, yet had never before been invited to India House. I told them that the reception was to recognise the fact that they were part of our history; whether for good or ill was for posterity to judge. I emphasised that our national movement was committed not to a doctrine but rather to a purpose – the modernisation of our society without loss of the Indian personality. It was gratifying for me to know that they, too, were looking more to the future than the past.

Today's India is a union of 27 states, bound by a constitution, which ensures full play to the regions without giving them the right to secede. The country has 14 national languages including the widely understood Hindi. In the past, democracy was taken chiefly to mean political democracy, roughly represented by the idea of every person having a vote. However, it is obvious that a vote by itself does not mean very much to a person who is starving. Therefore, political democracy by itself can only be valid when used to obtain a gradually increasing measure of economic democracy. That has been India's great endeavour, first through adopting a policy of self-sufficiency and now through opening the doors to the international market place.

Anthony Osmond-Evans' photography has captured the mood of this endeavour, and the determination of the people to achieve it. What is distinctive about this book is his perception of how time comes to a stop in India, and how monuments and people span the distance of ages to give the same message of cultural unity and solid defiance.

As Anthony has vividly demonstrated in this beautiful book, India represents a quest for spiritual fulfilment. Many outsiders tend to think that the country is lost in troubles and turbulence, but they miss the point. It is essential to concentrate not on India's problems but rather on its capacity to face them. Such a nation can never be defeated. It can withstand any vicissitudes, as it has demonstrated from time immemorial. Its strength is moral. People from all over the world should flock to see how India has preserved its ancient values, when other nations everywhere are being devoured by consumerism and pop culture. India is awake and stands firm on its feet.

The night has ended.
Put out the light of the lamp of thine own narrow corner
smudged with-smoke.
The great morning which is for all appears in the East.
Let its light reveal us to each other who walk on the same
path of pilgrimage.

RABINDRANATH TAGORE

13

INDIA

SRINIGAR

MANDI
AMRITSAR

DELHI

BIKANER
JAISALMER
JODHPUR
JAIPUR
AGRA
LUCKNOW
GWALIOR
VARANASI

GANGTOK
DARJEELING
GAUHATI
SHILLONG

UDAIPUR
KHAJURAHO

CALCUTTA

AHMADABAD
BARWANI
SURAT

NAGPUR

CUTTACK
BHUBANESWAR
KONARAK
PURI

**MUMBAI
(BOMBAY)**
AURANGABAD
POONA
HYDERABAD

GOA

BANGALORE
MADRAS

MYSORE
PONDICHERRY
COIMBATORE
MADURAI
COCHIN
ALEPPEY
TRIVANDRUM

1   km   1000 km

SCALE 1:15,000

Map outline taken from The Times Concise Atlas of The World 1985

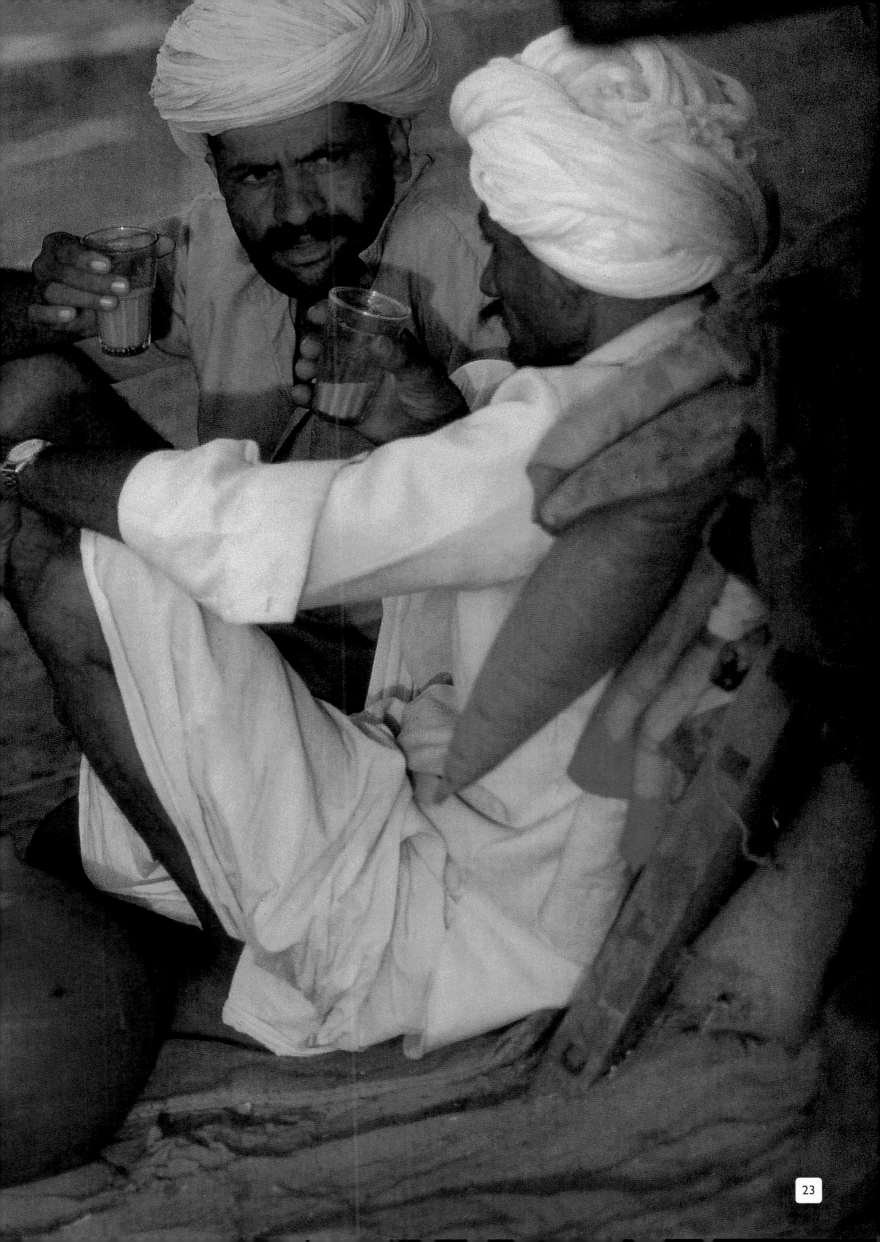

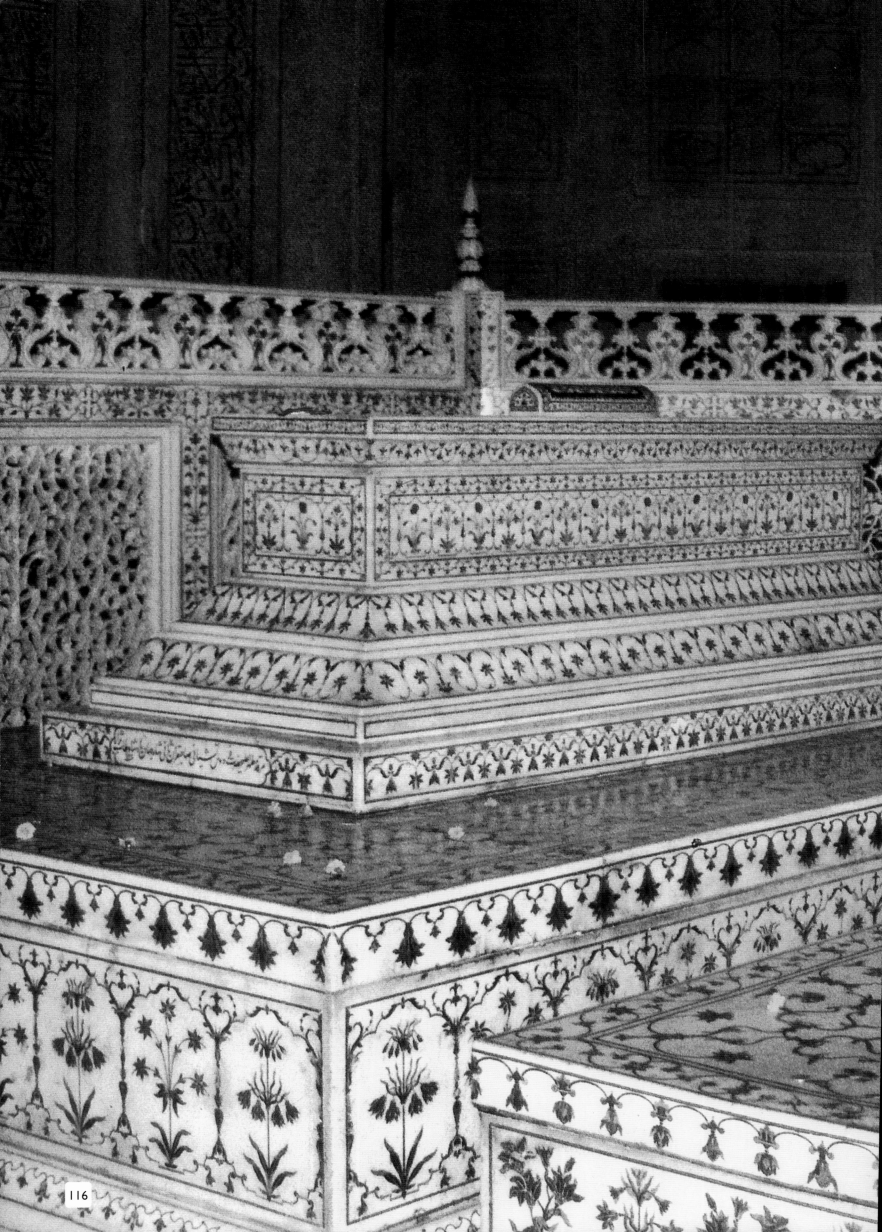

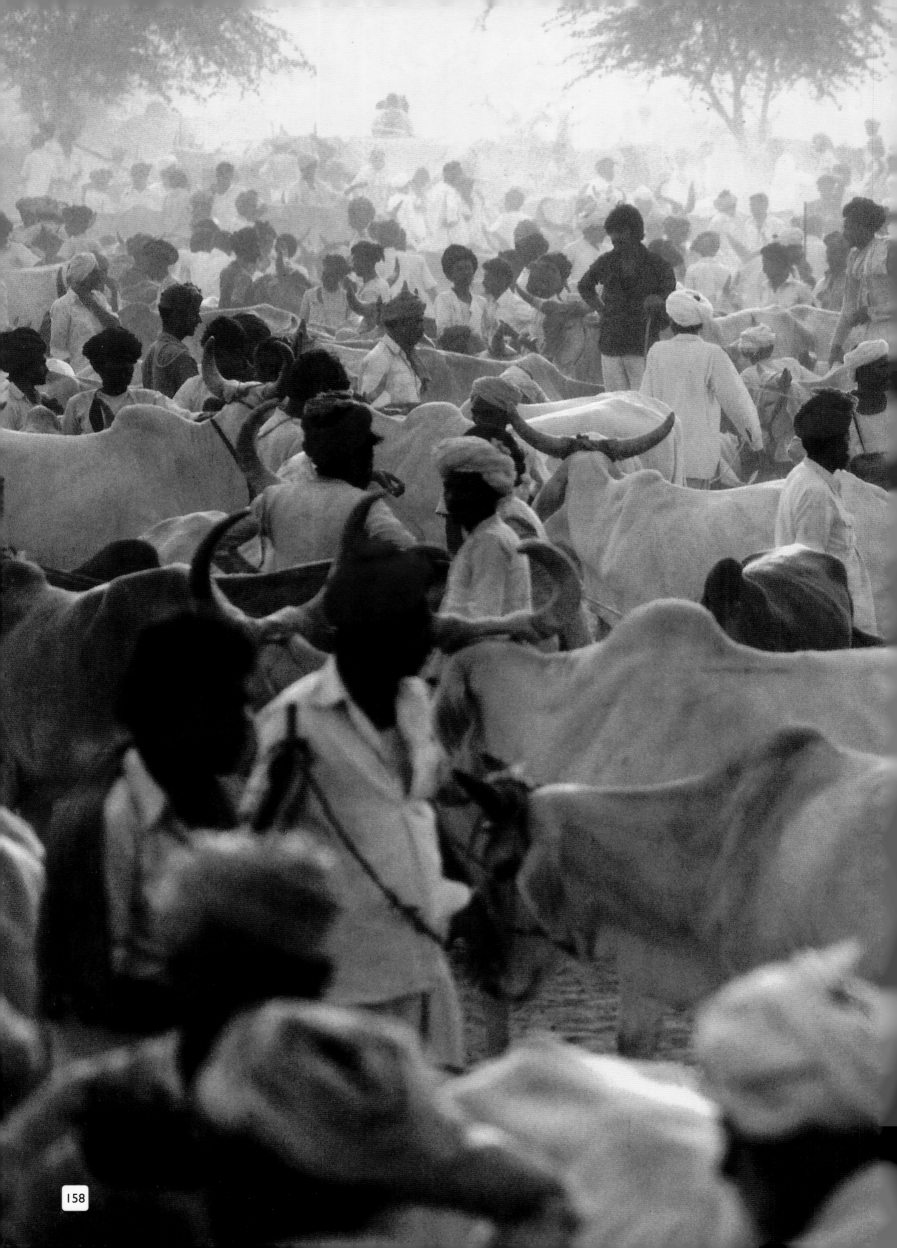

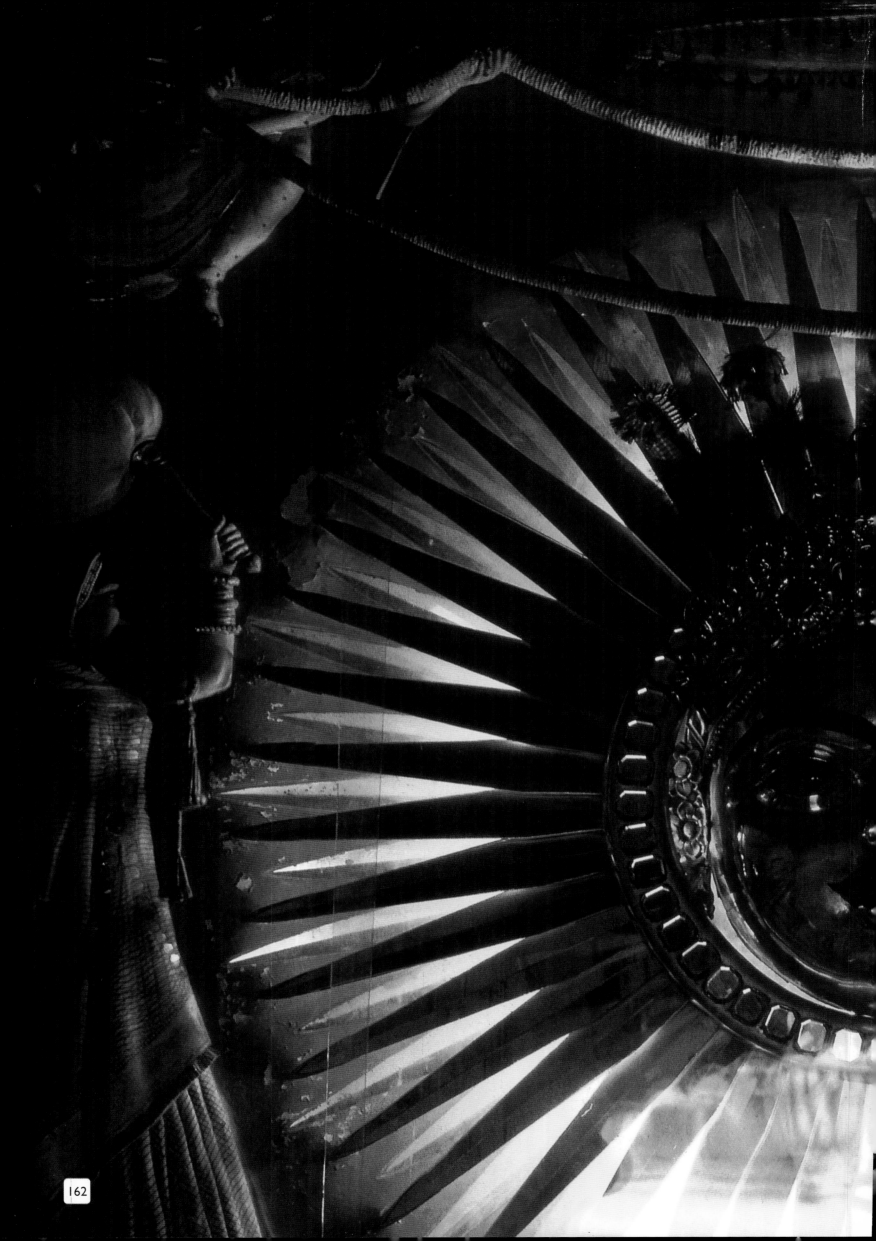

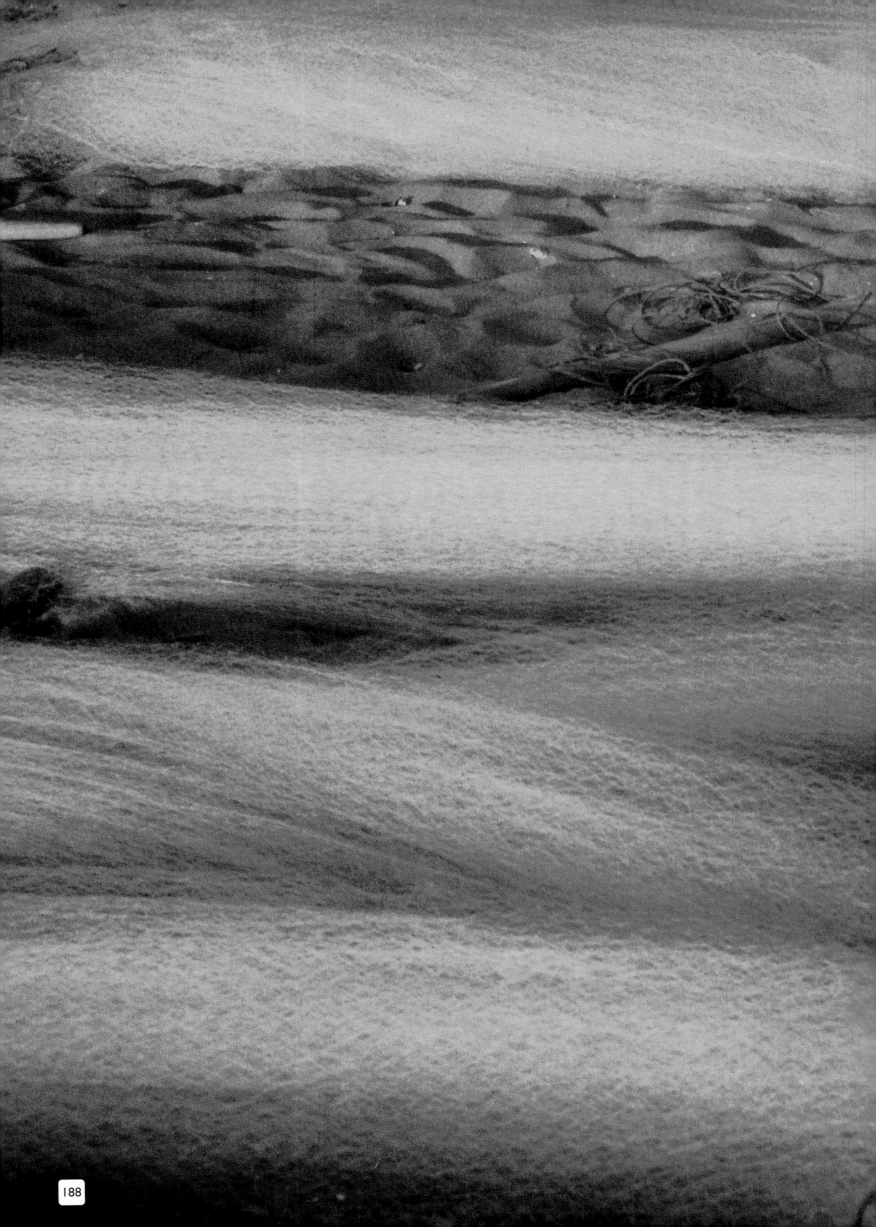

THE PHOTOGRAPHS

Title Page. Fatephur Sikri at dusk. The former capital of the Mughal Empire under the Emperor Akbar in the 16th century, it was abandoned, possibly for lack of water, and today is one of the most perfectly preserved 'ghost cities' in India. *Uttar Pradesh*

4. Ganesh, from the Pink Palace, Jaipur. The God of Wisdom and Mercy, the elephant-headed son of Siva and Parvati, is one of the most revered gods in the Hindu Pantheon. *Rajasthan*

6. A ceiling mural of Radha and Krishna in Dangarpur Palace.

7. The Lord Vishnu at the Meenakshi Temple, Madurai. *Tamil Nadu*

8/9. Mounted camels in the gathering dusk on the Lutyens designed ramparts, New Delhi. Below, the military band is playing Mahatma Gandhi's favourite British hymn, 'Abide With Me'.

10. August 15th 1947. A little boy wearing his Gandhi khadi oufit and Nehru hat celebrates the first day of Indian independence.

11. Silhouette of Mahatma Gandhi at the head of the Monument of the Eleven Martyrs, New Delhi.

13. A beautiful, mysterious lady in a traditional sari at a window in the Pink Palace, Jaipur. *Rajasthan*

15. This statue pays tribute to the Gurkha warrior. It stands before the tricolour flag of India in Darjeeling, with the Himalayas in the background. *West Bengal*

16. Traditional Odissi dancers from Konarak. *Orissa*

17. Snake charmer in Jaisalmer. *Rajasthan*.

18/19. A busy market at the Charminar Gate, in the heart of the Muslim Quarter of the old walled city of Hyderabad. The gate was built by Muhammad Quli Qutab Shah in 1591 to commemorate the end of a plague. *Andhra Pradesh*

20/21. Crowds at the annual Pushkar Camel Fair, which takes place in October/November. *Rajasthan*

22/23. The Pushkar Camel Fair. Camel dealers sip early morning tea and discuss the prices of camels and stock that are brought in to sell every Autumn. *Rajasthan*

24/25. Woman reels coloured threads for weaving in the Thar Desert. *Rajasthan*

26/27. Husking maize near spice villages in southern India. *Thekkady. Kerala*

28. Young Muslim girl from the Dharavi district. *Mumbai (Bombay)*

29. Fish being taken to market. *Goa*

30. A cheerful greeting from schoolboys in Lucknow. *Uttar Pradesh*

31. A young woman cleans oysters. *Goa*

32. As many as ten children crowd a bicycle rickshaw on their way home from school in Lucknow. *Uttar Pradesh*

33. Two little sisters from Tibet pose shyly for the camera. They now have a happy home in Darjeeling. *West Bengal*

34. Holy man. *Rajasthan*

35. Holy man on the steps of a ghat at Varanasi (Benares). One of the world's oldest cities and a place of pilgrimage for over 2,500 years, Varanasi is on the banks of the Ganges. Siva is said to have made his permanent home here since the dawn of creation. *Uttar Pradesh*

36. Embers of the dying Sun add lustre to a flute player at the Sun Temple at Konarak. The temple is thought to have been built by the Orissan king Narashimhadev I in the 13th century. The temple complex was dedicated to the Sun God, Surya. *Orissa*

37. A beautiful young woman is arrayed in Gold embroidered silk. Many consider Deepam of Bangalore to be India's finest purveyor of silk. *Karnataka*

38. A 'banjara' or nomad woman. She may have no permanent home, which is why she wears all her wealth. *Rajasthan*

39. Nimble fingers wrap a pinch of tobacco in a leaf to make a 'beedi'. The cheap handmade cheroots are smoked throughout India, and a high percentage are mass produced by families in the villages around Mangalore, *Karnataka*

40. Temple sculpture, Bhubaneswar. *Orissa*

41. One of a pair of silver urns, each with a capacity of 8,192 litres (1,802 gallons). Used for transporting holy Ganga water to England, when Madhn Singh II attended the Coronation of King Edward VII in 1902. The former Maharajah of Jaipur also considered that British water was unsuitable to drink! Pink Palace, Jaipur. *Rajasthan*

42/43. A group of villagers visit the City Palace, Udaipur, the splendid home of the Maharanas of Mewar. *Rajasthan*

44. A bridegroom, his face partly hidden by hanging strings of pearls and beads, displays a garland of currency notes pinned to his chest for good luck.

45. Holy man with beads. *Rajasthan*

46/47. Basket making in Udaipur. *Rajasthan*

48. Nuns at the entrance of Mother Teresa's mission in Calcutta, where she also lives.

49. Mother Teresa of Calcutta.

50. Schoolgirls hand in hand in Rajasthan

51. Greetings from a dye maker in Mandawa. *Rajasthan*

52. Dusk; smoke fills the air along the ghats at the holy city of Hardwar as thousands of pilgrims cook supper on tiny stoves. *Uttar Pradesh*

53. Dawn; a burnt offering before Buddhist prayer flags on a mountain near Gangtok. *Sikkim*

54/55. At first light, a Buddhist monk gazes across the valley at Kachenjunga, one of the world's highest mountains, in the Himalayas. *Sikkim*

56/57. Blue painted houses, viewed from Meherangarh Port, Jodhpur. The colour of the houses distinguishes them as being owned by Brahmins. *Rajasthan*

58/59. Rickshaws at dawn waiting for business at Lucknow's railway station. *Uttar Pradesh*

60/61. Lady in red, Jaisalmer. *Rajasthan*

62. According to the great poet, Rabindranath Tagore, "Every child comes with the message that God is still not discouraged of man". A Small boy from Anjar. *Gujarat*

63. Commemorative plaque at Jaisalmer's Fort. Dedicated to 300 courageous Bhatti Rajput women who, during the reign of Alauddin Khiji (1296-1316), chose self immolation ('jauhar') on a giant funeral pyre to avoid being violated by attacking Mughals. *Uttar Pradesh*

64. A Sadhu (holy man), covered in ash, reads scriptures at a pathside shrine on the pilgrims' route to Kedarnath, in the Himalayan foothills. *Uttar Pradesh*

65. The Nandi (Siva's Bull), on the Chamundi Hill, Mysore. Carved out of solid rock, and over 4.6 metres (15 feet) high, this is one of the largest statues of its kind in India. It is always garlanded in flowers and is constantly visited by pilgrims. *Karnataka*

66/67. Muslims at prayer ('namaz').

68/69. Hindus from all over India trek to the source of the Mother Ganges, just upstream from the tiny village of Gangotri, 3,140 metres (10,300 feet) above sea level. Here, many will collect a small container of the holy river's waters to take home as a sacred souvenir of their pilgimage. *Uttar Pradesh*

70/71. Hindus take a dip in the Ganges, high in the mountains near the source, believing that the waters of the holy river will purify them of their worldly sins. *Uttar Pradesh*

72/73. The fragile appearance of this bamboo bridge belies its real strength in withstanding the violent torrents of the mountain river. *Sikkim*

74/75. Periyar Lake at dawn. A family of wild elephants crosses the bow of the author's boat. The lake is part of India's oldest wildlife sanctuary, founded in 1934 under the Maharajah of Travancore. *Kerala*

76/77. Varanasi. Ritual washing by devotees at sunrise on the ghats of the sacred River Ganges. Hindus often refer to the city as 'Kashi', the 'City of Light', because of the golden glow of the temples and ghats in the early morning. Although the Ganges is the river of life, it is also thought to be an auspicious place to die. The ashes of deceased Hindus, including many from overseas, are consigned to its waters. *Utter Pradesh*

78. A perplexed small boy in a Gangtok monastery. He is not yet old enough to understand the text of the sacred book that has been placed in front of him by young novitiate monks. *Sikkim*

79. A child deep in her own thoughts at the Pushkar Camel Fair. *Rajasthan*

80. Young women changing costumes at the Pushkar Camel Fair. *Rajasthan*

81. This beautiful young woman is wearing the characteristic jewellery of the region. *Rajasthan*

82/83. Child with candles.

84/85. Chinese fishing nets at sunset near Fort Cochin. They are a reminder of early links with fishermen from imperial China. *Kerala*

86/87. Cochinese fishermen haul op their Chinese fishing nets at twilight. *Kerala*

88/89. Kathakali theatrical performance. This picture was taken in the middle of the night during a mystical ceremony in a remote and atmosphere laden temple, somewhere between the backwaters of Alleppey and the Coconut Lagoon. *Kerala*

90/91. Fire dancing in Cochin. Fart of a martial arts performance. A ten second time exposure reveals the circles formed by the artiste's handling of a flaming torch. Note his moving feet. *Kerala*

92. The Gomti River, Lucknow, at sunset. The river is a subsidiary of the Ganges. *Utter Pradesh*

93. Young woman at sunset, within the Palace of Jaipur. *Rajasthan*

94. The roof of this part of the Meenakshi temple complex at Madurai has recently been regilded. The temple, one of the largest and most impressive in India, is dedicated to Siva and his consort, 'the fisheyed' goddess

Meenakshi. The name Madurai is a corruption of 'mathuram' (nectar), and was given to the city after a drop of nectar fell here from Siva's hair. *Tamil Nadu*

95. Detail of a wall painting from Ajanta, near Aurangabad. The 30 caves there were carved from within the solid rock and decorated by Buddhist monks between 200 BC and 600 AD. *Maharashtra*

96. This graceful 12-year-old village girl carries a heavy sack of maize with the grace of a princess. *Rajasthan*

97. Old man with pugree.

98. Catching up with the news. *Rajasthan*

99. An old man relaxes with his hookah. *Rajasthan*

100/101. At the end of the day with bales of cotton ready for market, Aurangabad. *Maharashtra*

102. Chopping wood at Cuttack, the old state capital. This is no more than a 'boundary' away from the first class cricket ground that was used during the recent World Cup. *Orissa*

103. Woman milking, Mysore. *Karnataka*

104/105. Elephants waiting to take visitors up to Amber Fort, established by Rajah Man Singh in 1592. *Rajasthan*

106/107. This temple elephant may be found next to the Thousand Column Hall within the Meenakshi Temple at Madorai. Here he is about to give one of his 'daily blessings' with his trunk in exchange for gifts of food and money. *Tamil Nadu*

108. This Jaisalmer street boasts the finest traditional 'havelis' or residences in India. Strategically placed on the spice route from India to Central Asia, Jaisalmer's merchants vied with each other to build the most elaborate havelis and to employ the best 'silavats' (stone carvers). *Rajasthan*

109. The Sun Temple, Konarak. The temple is here seen patrolled by a crescent moon at night. It was originally conceived as the Sun God's own chariot standing on 12 pairs of eight-spoke wheels and drawn by seven horses. *Orissa*

110. Swing made for a prince of Jaipur. *Rajasthan*

111. Interior of the 16th-century Seth Bhandashah Jain Temple, Bikaner. *Rajasthan*

112. A passing elephant casts her shadow. *Rajasthan*

113. The first pink fingers of dawn touch the Taj Mahal at Agra, the most beautiful building in the world. This was Shah Jahan's homage to his favourite queen, Mumtaz-i-Mahal, who died giving birth to their 14th child in 1629. Shah Jahan died in 1666. Over 20,000 people worked on the construction from 1631 to 1653, including experts from Persia, France and Italy. *Uttar Pradesh*

114/115. The Taj Mahal at dusk the same day, from the rooftop of the nearby Red Fort. The whole character of this marble building alters as the light changes and it is worth several visits to appreciate its extraordinary beauty. The entire complex has been built within an integral architectural plan representing a formalised Islamic view of Paradise, incorporating lush gardens, water courses, gates, surrounding walls and a mosque - with the mausoleum at the centre. *Uttar Pradesh*

116/117. The inlaid marble tombs of Shah Jahan and his wife Mumtaz are profusely decorated with inlaid flowers, each composed of as many as 60 cut precious stones. Both are buried, in accordance with Muslim law, seven feet underground. On all higher levels there is a replica of each tombstone, so that no one shall walk over the grave itself. *Uttar Pradesh*

118/119. The Grand Entrance Hall of the Palace of Mysore, which was rebuilt in 1907, the seat of Mr Wodeyar, the former Maharajah. The procession at the Dussehra Festival, which usually takes place during October, passes near here and the priceless jewel-studded gold throne is put on display. *Karnataka*

120/121. Ajanta cave, one of 130. Skillfully carved out of rock. Aurangaba. *Maharashtra*

122/123. Dawn rises at the 54-metre (177 feet) high Lingaraj Temple at Bhubaneswar which was completed in the early 11th century. Also known as the Temple of Bhubeneshwara or the Lord of the Universe. It is off limits to all non-Hindus. The whole temple complex is 150 square metres (1,600 square feet) and is dominated by a 40-metre-high (131 feet) tower. *Orissa*

124/125. The frenzy of the Rath Yatra Festival at Puri, one of India's four holiest cities. At midsummer the gods leave their temple in their chariots. Lord Jagannath, Lord of the Universe and incarnation of Vishnu, commemorates the journey of Krishna on a gigantic canopied chariot (the origin of the English word 'juggernaut'), 14 metres (45 feet) high and 10 metres (32 feet) wide, on 16 wheels each more than two metres in diameter. Hundreds of thousands of pilgrims vie for the honour of pulling the chariots. In the past devotees would often throw themselves under the wheels in order to die in God's sight. *Orissa*

126. Mehandi Night. Applying mehandi henna to a young woman's hand before a wedding.

127. A local schoolgirl in Varanasi. She is colourfully decorated for her part in a play about the life of Lord Krishna. *Uttar Pradesh*

128. Gold masks at a ceremony in the Kulu Valley. Himchal Pradesh

129. The Temple of Trambakeshwar. The Golden Mask of Siva weighing 8.5 kilos of gold with its 5.5 kilo golden crown is encrusted with more than 2,000 rubies, pearls, emeralds and diamonds. It was presented by the early Maratha Kings.

130/131. The children of two prominent Indian diamond merchant families glance lovingly at each other during their wedding in Mumbai (Bombay). There were over 10,000 guests in the lavishly decorated football stadium. *Maharashtra*

132/133. The former Maharajah of Jodhpur, Gat Singh, an Old Etonian, and his son on their way to prayers to celebrate his birthday. Rajasthan

134/135. Military band at the Republic Day procession in New Delhi.

136/137. Pot vendor's stall, Jaisalmer. Note the classic, age-old shape of the water pots. *Rajasthan*

138/139. Relief at the Lakshmana Temple, one of several important temples at Khajuraho. Built during the Chandalla period during the 10th century, this temple is dedicated to Vishnu. It also incorporates Apsara', heavenly dancing nymphs and 'Mithuna', sensuously carved erotic figures. *Madhaya Pradesh*

140/141. Jostling onions in the vegetable market, Mysore. *Karnataka*

142. Dhobis (washermen) at the Dhobi Ghat. This is the Mumbai (Bombay) Public Laundry, where for generations, laundry families have been allocated their own area in which to undertake different types of laundry. *Maharashtra*

143. Typical Muslim dish, which includes chili, yoghurt and coriander. It is served at Id (the end of Ramadan) by a street vendor near the Charminar Gate, Hyderabad. *Andhra Pradesh*

144. A young Chittal stag, nearly full grown, shows his velvet antlers at first light in the jungle of Khana National Park, near Nagpur, which is virtually in the centre of India. This is one of the favourite foods of the Bengal tiger. Overhead, screeching monkeys warn of danger. *Maharashtra*

145. Coconut plantation workers with a bullock cart in the plain below Kodaikanal. This is a most beautiful hill station, much favoured during the hottest weather by the Raj and used by wealthy Indians today. *Tamil Nadu*

146/147. Tea plantation in the hills, a two-hour drive from Cochin. Tea pickers carry in the fruits of their labours before breaking for lunch. *Kerala*

148/149. Once a year in August, the Nehru Cup Snake Boat Race takes place at Alleppey, a small market town built round a maze of canals. These are practice races held in February. *Kerala*

150/151. Small temple reflected in a lake near Bhubaneswar. *Orissa*

152/153. Women picking chrysanthemums for garlands. *Rajasthan*

154/155. A charming tea picker gives a welcoming smile on a tea estate near the Brahmaputra River. Kaziranga. *Assam*

156/157. This wonderfully colourful market in Varanasi, with its onions, carrots, coriander, ginger, chilis, peppers, cabbages, tomatoes and aubergines, is a pleasant change from the crowded pilgrimage sites of the Ganges. *Uttar Pradesh*

158/159. Distinctive red turbans add emphasis where countless animals kick up a dusty haze at the annual cattle market in Sanchor on the edge of the deserts of western Rajasthan.

160. This handsome old man was the centre of attention in an Udaipur street. *Rajasthan*

161. Close-up of a Kathakali performer who, having applied makeup, inserts an eggplant flower under the eyelid to redden it. India's most spectacular dance drama originated some 500 years ago. It incorporates elements of yoga and ayurvedic (traditional Indian) medicine.

162/163. The Shiv Niwas Palace Museum, Udaipur. The Sun is the emblem of the Suryanan, the 'Solar Dynasty' rulers of Udaipur. The statues are lifesize. *Rajasthan*

164/165. Shiv Niwas Palace, Udaipur, at night. *Rajasthan*

166/167. The Shivalingam (symbol of male virility) Shrine at Elephanta Island. The caves are thought to have been excavated between 450 and 750 AD. *Mumbai (Bombay)*

168/169. Fishermen putting out to sea, Kovalam. *Kerala*

170. A farmer washes under an irrigation pipe after a hard day's toil in the fields. *Rajasthan*

171. Tara, the elephant made internationally famous by the author Mark Shand, who rode her 500 miles through India in a lake near Kipling Camp, Khana National Park, near Nagpur, which is in the centre of India. *Maharashtra*

172/173. The famous Sikh Temple, Swarnmandir, the Golden Temple at Amritsar. The religious seat of the Sikh religion, and its holiest shrine, is also known as the Hari Mandir. It was built in the 16th century, destroyed in 1761 and rebuilt in 1764. The golden dome is said to he covered with 100 kg of pure gold and is supposed to represent an inverted lotus flower symbolising the Sikh's concern for the problems of this world. *Punjab*

174. An attendant at the Palace of Jodhpur. Note the vultures on the parapet behind. *Rajasthan*

175. Arched entrance to Neemrana Fortress. Two hours' drive from Delhi, the fortress has been converted into a hotel, tastefully preserving all the old traditions. *Rajasthan*

176. Making sandalwood paste within a Jain temple at Jaisalmer. *Rajasthan*

177. At ease on duty, a guard reads his paper at Jaipur's City Palace. Also known as the Pink Palace, it covers one seventh of the total area of the meticulously planned 18th-century walled city. It was Maharajah Ram Singh 11(1835-80) who painted Jaipur pink as a sign of welcome to the Prince of Wales (later King Edward VII). *Rajasthan*

178. Rajput dancer, Jaipur. *Rajasthan*

179.   (a) Torchbearer, Mandawa. *Rajasthan*

(b) Dressing and fastidiously making-up
for a performance of Kathakali takes several hours.
The epic dances were originally temple dances, which
told the story of Ramayana and Mahabharata. Cochin.
Kerala

180. Colourful pyramids of ground spices,
including turmeric, garlic and coriander, give forth a
heady mix of aromas. *Rajasthan*

181. On the ghats of Varanasi, a young woman
about to immerse herself in the Ganges for her dawn
wash. *Uttar Pradesh*

182/183. A rich tableau is provided by the women
taking their loads to be weighed, near Barwani, after a
long day picking chilis in the fields. *Madhya Pradesh*

184/185. Dawn at the Flower Market in Calcutta.
Today's fresh marigold garlands contrast with the
detritus of yesterday.

186. It is said that travelling by train in India is
more than a nostalgic return to the great days of
steam. The Indian Railway system, with its 62,000
kilometres (38,750 miles) of track, is the world's fourth
largest. With its 1.6 million employees, it is the world's
biggest employer. Every day 11,000 trains carry ten
million passengers to and from 7,000 stations. This
train was pictured in Rajasthan.

187. A Tibetan refugee smiles for the photographer
whilst laying asphalt. Gangtok. *Sikkim*

188/189. Networking! A Fisherman repairs his nets
at dawn. Puri. *Orissa*

190/91. Camel caravan at sunset, Jaisalmer.
Rajasthan

192. Elephants at dawn near India's border with
Nepal.

The Photographers

The majority of the photographs in this book were
taken by Anthony Osmond-Evans.

Additional photography by:

Julian Bubb	34;45;46/47;81;98;99;108;132/133;180
Gina Corrigan	7;22/23;24/25;38;41;62;97;148/149;
	156/157;168; 179b
Deepam	37
Ashok Dilwali	44
Lorraine Felkin	78;93;96; 181
Prakash Israni	116/117;138/139
Samar Joda	112
Doctor R K V Katrecha	6, 129
M L Mehta	66/67;126;128;134/135;188/189
Kim Naylor	28;42/43;52;64;68/69;70/71;
	127;158/159;177;182/183
Tikku Pawan (STC)	92
Vishnu Punjabi	95
Anand K. Razdan (STC)	172/173
T S Satyan	20/21;79;80;161
Stock Transparency Services	124/125
Colin Wade	29

Acknowledgements

HE Dr L M Singhvi
The High Commissioner for India in London

HE Sir David Gore-Booth KCMG
The British High Commissioner at New Delhi

Kuldip Nayar - for his foreword and wise advice

Dr S K Arora, Attache (Hindi and Culture), the Office
of the High Commissioner for India

For their skills and help:
    Richard Johnson - Design
    George Metcalfe, Harvard Business Group - Editorial

Administrative Assistance:
    Sue Jobson
    Jean Jones and Don McGregor of Good Connections
    Sue Garfield and Sharon Feldman-Vazan of
        The Organisers
    Julie van der Vliet of Accu-Rapid

Photographic Assistance
    Kodak Professional - European African & Middle
    East Region:
    Fred Heigold - General Manager
    Keith Purves - General Manager (SEMA)
    John Creighton - Business Support Manager (SEMA)
    Humayun Dhanrajgir - General Manager, Kodak,
    India
    Amal Jajodia - Kodak Professional Country Manager,
    India
    Barney Servis at Optikos

Photographic Equipment
    Mamiya

Permission to use the portrait of Anthony Osmond-Evans
    Sir David English, Chairman,
    Associated Newspapers

Travel
    Mary-Anne Denison-Pender of Cox & Kings
    Zakria - our principal driver in India
    Gerard Guerrini

Special Mention
    Captain Singh of the New Delhi Police who was there
    Herr Östereichfeder who was not all there

Published in 2004 by Mercury Books London
20 Bloomsbury Street, London WC1B 3JH

Cover Design by Open Door Limited, Rutland, UK

Title: INDIA THE BEAUTIFUL

ISBN: 1 904668 48 8